DAVID HAUTZIG

At the Supermarket

ORCHARD BOOKS
New York

To Susan Cohen—
... started in children's books,
my mother told me to get a good agent.
I didn't listen to my mother.
I got the best agent.

Thanks to Claire D'Amour and
everybody at The Big Y, The Photo Shop
in Pittsfield, and Harold Underdown,
the real "father" of this book.

ORCHARD BOOKS • 95 MADISON AVENUE • NEW YORK, NY 10016
Manufactured in the United States of America
Printed by Barton Press, Inc. Bound by Horowitz/Rae.
Book design by Antler & Baldwin Design Group

10 9 8 7 6 5 4 3 2 1
The text of this book is set in 13.5 point New Century Schoolbook.
The illustrations are full-color photographs.

Library of Congress Cataloging-in-Publication Data
Hautzig, David.
        At the supermarket / written and photographed by David Hautzig.
        p. cm.
        ISBN 0-531-06832-3. — ISBN 0-531-08682-8 (lib. bdg.)
        1. Supermarkets—Juvenile literature. [1. Supermarkets.]
    I. Title.
HF5469.H38 1994   381'. 148—dc20   93-26976

A supermarket never goes to sleep. Every minute of every day, somebody is working at The Big Y supermarket in Pittsfield, Massachusetts. Men and women fill the shelves with all the "stuff" we see every day at the supermarket— fruits, vegetables, boxes of cereal, canned soup, and pints of ice cream. Others may be unloading a truck of fresh fish or preparing cuts of meat. People are busy all the time. Let's start at 6:00 A.M. and watch for a day to see how the supermarket works.

The store doesn't open to customers for another hour, but the work day at The Big Y is well under way. A truck carrying fresh milk and eggs arrives at the Dairy and Frozen Foods department. The delivery person unloads his cargo into a giant refrigerator.

During the day, while customers take milk and eggs, Shane refills the shelves constantly. The back of the milk shelves is actually part of the refrigerator.

Another truck arrives with boxes of fresh apples, oranges, bananas, tomatoes, peppers, lettuce, and all sorts of other fruits and vegetables for the Produce department. Steve and Bob move the boxes on a "hi-jack" into the produce cooler, another giant refrigerator.

Like the milk and eggs, fruits and vegetables don't stay in their refrigerator very long. Steve and Bob soon put them out on the shelves so the customers can buy the freshest produce possible.

All the produce that arrives this morning will be on the shelves or already sold by dinnertime. The supermarket gives fruits and vegetables that have been on the shelves for more than two days to a local food bank for the poor.

Soon, the *Seafood* truck arrives, carrying salmon, flounder, shrimp, tuna, and other fresh fish. Robert prepares the fish counter for the day while the truck is being unloaded. He fills it with ice to keep the fish fresh.

The fish must be sold the same day, or it gets thrown out. If fish is not eaten when it is fresh, it can make a person sick.

7:00 AM

The store opens to customers at 7:00 A.M., and trucks carrying the Packaged Bakery items begin to arrive. They bring the breads, cakes, and cookies that are not baked in the store. In this part of the supermarket, the people driving the truck also unload it and put the fresh baked goods onto the shelves. At the same time, they remove breads and cakes that have been on the shelves too long. The older baked goods (only a few days old) go to a food bank. There are many different companies that bake bread and cakes, and each one sends its own truck. All morning long, you can find somebody putting fresh bread on the shelf in the packaged bakery section.

Soda and snack foods like potato chips and pretzels are also handled by the delivery people. Every day, the Pepsi person comes to The Big Y and fills the shelves with the different Pepsi products.

Why is there always so much "stuff" at the supermarket? It hardly ever runs out of anything. One reason is the store's warehouse in back, stocked with many items ready to be brought out when needed.

The heads of all the different departments at The Big Y also check every day to see what they need. If they notice they are running out of something, they make sure they get more for the next day. Richard, head of the Produce department, sees that many green peppers have been sold and that he should order some. So he writes down the special code number for green peppers, and the numbers for any other produce his department needs, in his order book.

He punches all the code numbers in his order book into a machine at his desk called an MSI. Then he hooks up the MSI to the phone and sends the order to a big computer at the company's main warehouse. The computer can then tell people in the main warehouse what Richard needs. Tomorrow, green peppers will be on the truck delivering to the produce department.

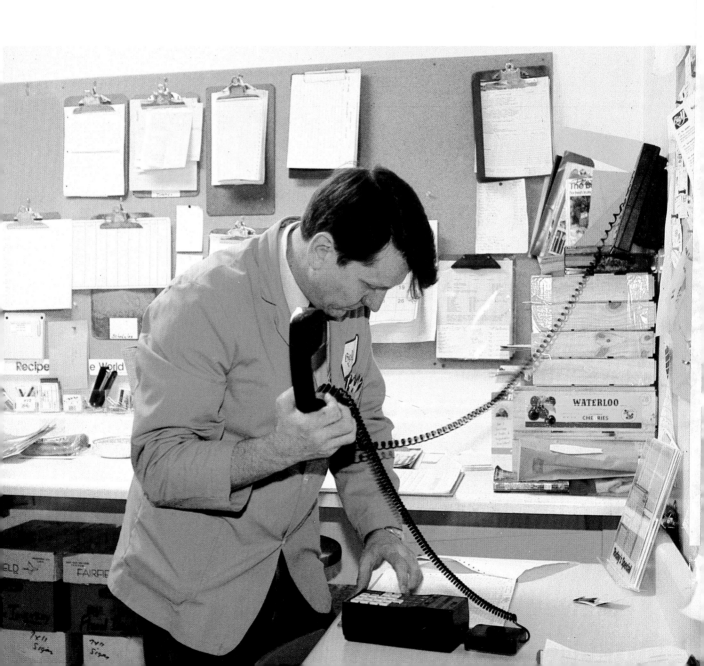

The produce department also has a **Salad Bar** of fresh vegetables and prepared foods like potato salad. When the produce truck rolls in every morning, some of the fresh fruits and vegetables are set aside for the salad bar.

Julie washes them, cuts them up, and puts them into separate bowls. Julie fills the salad bar case with ice to keep the vegetables and salads fresh, and then lays out large silver bowls filled with that day's choices. At lunchtime, the salad bar gets very crowded with people who work near The Big Y.

The meat, deli, and bakery departments all receive and unload their deliveries late in the morning.

The meat truck delivers many different types of meat to the Meat department every day, but the most popular are beef, chicken, and turkey.

All beef starts out as big pieces called primals. Dave divides up these big pieces either by hand or with a big machine called a band saw into different "cuts" like steaks or roasts. Rob runs beef through the meat grinder to make hamburger meat.

The workers then put the cut or ground beef onto Styrofoam trays. Chicken and turkey come to the store already cut up or ground and on trays. Linda sends each one through a machine that weighs the tray of meat, wraps plastic around it, and puts a sticker with the price on the plastic wrap.

Lisa takes the wrapped meat out to the meat department shelves for people to buy. All the meat that comes in on the 11:00 A.M. truck will be on the shelves by suppertime.

On the same truck with the beef, chicken, and turkey come the meats used by the Deli department. These are already cooked meats, like bologna, ham, and roast beef, in big rolls called loaves. They go into the deli case along with loaves of different cheeses, like Swiss, American, and provolone. Like the salad bar, the deli department is very busy at lunchtime. People buy sandwiches made with whatever they want.

The dough used by the Bakery to make bread, rolls, cakes, and cookies comes to the supermarket frozen. Travis puts this dough onto pans, a job called panning the dough. Travis then rolls the pans into a cooler so the dough can thaw (the thawing takes most of the day, so we'll come back to the bakery later).

All through the day, people come into The Big Y to get the food they need, and then take it to the **Cashiers** to pay for it. The cashiers have a special machine called a bar code reader that helps them quickly add up the cost of a person's groceries. Most items in the supermarket have a bar code somewhere on their packaging. The bar code reader can "read" this with a beam of light and tell the cash register how much the item costs. This is quicker than if the cashier had to punch in each price on his or her register.

The **Dairy and Frozen Foods** department gets a second delivery in the afternoon. Cases of cheese and butter go into a big refrigerator, and ice cream and frozen dinners go into a freezer to be kept cold. From there, Shane and Jeff take whatever is needed out to the display coolers and freezers.

Frozen foods can stay in a freezer for a *very* long time and still be okay to eat. But that's not true for dairy foods like milk and cheese. They stay good for eating only a short time. So every item in the dairy section comes in with a date stamped on the package. This date is the last date the item may be sold by the supermarket. After that, it has to be taken off the shelf.

9:00 PM

The *Grocery* department gets the last and biggest delivery of the day in the evening. Almost three thousand cases of food and other items in cans, bottles, and boxes come in every day. The grocery department takes up more than half of The Big Y.

First, workers take the cases from the truck out onto the supermarket floor. At 10:00 P.M., when the supermarket closes to customers, a seven-person overnight crew arrives. They stay in the store all night to unpack the three thousand boxes and get the store ready for the next day.

The crew first places each box by the shelf where that item goes. Jim and the others on the overnight crew then open the boxes up. Jim uses a pricing gun to put a sticker with that item's price on each can, box, or bottle. Usually, the crew prices about 72,000 items and then puts them on the shelves.

The **Bakery** now swings back into action. The breads and rolls that were thawing in the cooler are now soft and "doughy." So Lori rolls the trays into the proofer, which is like an oven but not as hot. It uses steam to heat the dough lightly so that the yeast in it will grow faster and make it puff up. After the dough rises, Lori moves it into the oven, which can handle sixty pans at a time, for baking. Once all the baked goods are done and have cooled down, they are put either into plastic bags or into cardboard boxes and placed on shelves for customers to buy when the store reopens.

Back in the **Grocery** department, the overnight crew is just finishing putting things onto the shelves. The store will open in just two hours, and it's time for blocking and leveling. Jim and the others turn every item on every shelf, so that the name faces the front, and line them all up at the front of the shelf. This way, every item sold in the supermarket can easily be seen by the customers.

5:00 AM

A new day is beginning at The Big Y. Fresh fruits and vegetables are arriving at the produce department, fresh milk and eggs are going into the big refrigerator in dairy and frozen foods, and fresh bread will soon be on the shelves in the packaged bakery area.

Supermarkets never sleep because people depend on them for the food they eat and the things that make their everyday lives comfortable.